D1492871

First published in 2010 by:

Live It Publishing
27 Old Gloucester Road
London, United Kingdom.
WC1N 3AX
www.liveitpublishing.com

ISBN 978-1-906954-15-4 (pbk)

DEDICATED

To Mum, Dad and David.

With thanks to Jeanette.

DEDICATED

1

A Brief Introduction

Suddenly, I was wide awake. It was dark outside but the street lights were illuminating the bedroom. I looked across the bedroom to where my brother, David, was sleeping in his bed. The whole house was silent so I knew my parents had gone to bed and were probably asleep, but what had woken me up? Why was I suddenly wide awake? I was looking around when at the doorway I saw two black robed monks with their hoods up. They walked past our bedroom door, I instantly froze to the spot, too scared to murmur a single word, I pulled my blankets up to just under my bulging eyeballs, and that's how I eventually fell asleep.

I was eight years old and this was not the first time I had encountered spirit.

The reason I had seen the monks that night didn't make sense to me then, but it certainly would do later on in life. I still think back to that night and can see those two monks as clear now in my mind's eye as I could then.

I've always known that I didn't view life and our world the same as most people did, as a little girl I always felt

this, I knew if I hadn't had a very good day at school, or I was feeling down, my spirit friend (which I now know as my door keeper) would always be there to talk to.

Your door keeper is your main spirit guide, they are with you from birth until death, and everyone has a door keeper whether they are aware of them or not.

We can all talk to our door keepers, and ask them for guidance within our lives, when you talk to them you need to talk to them as if you are talking to yourself. You can do this out loud or inside your head, then just listen or feel within yourself and the first answer you hear or feel will be the correct one. Don't try too hard as communication can feel very subtle at times and stronger at other times, you will usually get it stronger when you fail to listen to them the first time, sometimes it is just like a feeling or passing thought. I really do believe that they do try their hardest to help and guide us when they can, but in the materialistic fast paced life in which we now live, we seem to be too preoccupied with our physical and material lives to listen to that inner voice, or take any notice of the subtle communication we receive and just like some people now, I didn't always listen.

There are more within these pages later on that will help you to discover who your door keeper is and to strike up a stronger relationship with them. Some people feel it is important to remember that our guardian angel also plays an equally large part in our lives, they too walk by the side of us

2

Farewell to David

I recall that when I was about eight years old, I went to my first funeral, it was the funeral of my Nanny Holden, she was my great Nan really, she had bought up my Dad from an early age. Dad's father passed to spirit when he was about six years old. l don't re-call ever having met my great Grandad, so l think he had either died or left before I ever went to my Nan's house.

Prior to her death we used to go and visit her as a family, usually once a week on a Saturday, and towards the end of her life she had a bed in the downstairs back room. I can't re-call too much about those days, only to say that I used to really like going over to see her. I do remember one thing though. She was a very stubborn and independent lady right up until the very end, despite the fact that she was bed ridden most of the time. She refused point blank to have any outside help. She didn't like strangers in her home. When she took a turn for the worse, she agreed to have extra help. My Dad said "that's it, she knows she won't last much longer, that's why she has agreed to extra help". Sure enough she was gone within no time, it's like she knew she was going and there was no point in fighting it anymore. She just accepted the inevitable and once she relaxed, she just faded gently and quietly.

About a week after her death, Nanny Holden's funeral was held. I remember seeing the coffin being carried out of the hearse and into the church, and thinking this feels very weird, all these people with sad looks on their faces and I didn't feel sad at all; because strangely enough it didn't feel like she had died, it almost felt like she was there with me. I know now I felt her spirit presence at the funeral.

Once the funeral was over we all went back to Nanny Holden's house. As I stepped into the doorway I knew I was right, I could feel her presence in the house. At this age, this really did feel weird, I couldn't quite grasp what I was really feeling, it was as if I was expecting her to be lying in her bed in the back room but when I walked into the backroom Nanny Holden wasn't there. Could it be that someone was helping her back from the toilet? No, she really had gone, even though I could feel her right by my side and I could hear her voice in my head, and I knew that this wasn't my imagination.

In later years my Dad used to say "you get your gift from your Nan", by which I knew he meant my great Nanny Holden, because I had never met my Dad's Mum. According to my Dad Nanny Holden knew about people and situations

it", as if to try and console me, but really I knew that it was David that had died, I had felt him go.

I was to find out later that I had felt his spirit leave his body at the exact time of death, but l kept thinking it can't be him he's only just fifteen years old, it was all I could do to stop myself from crying for the remainder of the afternoon until my parents came into the school. I really do think that my friend thought I had lost the plot that day. As soon as a teacher had entered my classroom about mid-afternoon to ask for me to go to the headmaster's office, I started to cry, before even entering the office I could feel my parent's pain. I was just thirteen and my whole world had been turned upside down.

Shortly after David's death he was moved to the chapel of rest in Highcliffe-on-Sea, which was a short distance from where we lived. Every day, and sometimes more than once a day, until David was buried, my Mum would go and see him, often with my Dad by her side, and every day she would say to me "you must go to see your brother, you need to go and say goodbye to him", until on the last day before his funeral I finally plucked up enough courage to go and see him. My friend came along with me for support, which I was so grateful for. As we entered the small, cold, emotionless room, there in front of us lay my brother David in an oak coffin. He looked just as if he was just sleeping. I almost expected him to jump up and shout "Boo!",

I've never been able to remember a lot of the next day, and I still don't, it's as if the brain click's in its safety mechanism and blocks certain things out. Part of what I do re-call is the amount of people and school mates of David's present in the cemetery, it all went to show how popular he was.

The days that followed were full of quiet sorrow, un-spoken words and silent glances. My Nan and Grandad said their goodbyes and headed off back to Birmingham, l really wished they had stayed longer.

There were several times in the coming weeks when Mum would take the dog for a walk, and not return for a number of hours. Dad and l would always go looking for her, we would look in the cemetery first, but she was never there, then after frantically looking everywhere for hours on end we would return to David's grave just to find her on her knee's weeping. They were difficult times.

Because David died half way through September, the first Christmas didn't exist at all. Shortly after we moved again to Worcestershire to be closer to Nan and Grandad. The hard times didn't seem to stop and give my parents a much needed breather at all, and o boy did l miss David! Even if it was just to argue with him. At times I felt very lonely, even though I still had my spirit friends, so l came to realise that l had my friends although l couldn't see them in the physical body, l could see their energies sometimes, and I always feel them by my side. I feel very comforted to have had their company at that time as it was them alone that helped to keep me sane.

where my friend Bobby would be, so I made my way up to the top of the house, which used to be used as one of the boy's dormitories in the days when the house had been a private boy's school.

Once up there I found Bobby sitting back in a chair enjoying a beer. We got chatting about what we had both been up to over that weekend, when, out of the corner of my eye, I saw a figure of a man floating back and forth in front of the huge window. My friend also saw something, but I think what he saw was more of an outline than anything else. Bobby was jumping up and down, pointing at the window and shouting "look, look", as I focused in more I could see that it was the spirit of a guy who was aged somewhere in his late twenties, wearing slacks and a shirt open part of the way down his chest, with true a 1970's style collar on it. He was of slim build and medium height, although I could not see his feet, his hair style was a typical style of the 1970's too, he seemed to have a blank expression on his face, to be totally honest at this point we legged it, because we knew that we were on the second floor of a very large house and that there was no way that any living person would be floating in front of the window like that, and there was no scaffolding up or any ledges. I knew all too well that it was this guy's spirit but unfortunately I didn't hang around to ask him what he'd come for, although I did get the feeling that he had taken his

that house in the next few years, from monks to estate workers, who I would get a glimpse of, or just a knowing that they were there, but I never felt the spirit of that particular guy there again.

Over the next few years I still seemed to pretty much get on with life, but spirit never left my side. On the whole most of the folks I hung around with were sound people. There were always one or two who would involve themselves in my life, and yes, we have all let them in (let's be honest now). Only I had learnt to take notice of what I was being told by spirit (well most of the time), for which I was very grateful. I believe that between my door keeper and my other spirit guides they kept me safe and tried very hard to guide me in the right direction and, believe me, they didn't have an easy job. I was what was known as wilful and that's putting it mildly

I still kept silent about what I classed as my friends (spirit), in case people thought I was weird. I started listening more to my inner voice/spirit, and started working on opening up my psychic abilities more. I used to take note of when someone would phone when I had been thinking of them, and them me, as I do believe and I have proved to myself first of all that thoughts are living things and they astral travel. Give it a go, put your thoughts out to a few people and see what happens.

I don't believe in coincidences - only a set of situations that further your life's path. Even if it's to teach you a certain lesson that you need to learn, or to bring you together with the people you need to be with, listen to your gut instinct. As the saying goes, act upon it or don't act upon it that's up to you as we all have free will, but just take a note of what happens either way, and you'll find that listening to your own gut instinct will serve you well. Going against this instinct will not, draw your own conclusions from this, but in my experience it is very interesting to see how certain things map out. You could practice with hunches to do with other people, see what happens, and see if your hunches were correct. I often knew what people were going to say before they said the words, the more I took notice of this the more it happened. I also somehow developed the art of knowing what people had said about me, although this sometimes wasn't good and I had to learn to keep this very much to myself, as people would have thought that I was paranoid, as I had not heard it said, but like anything, "The truth will out in the end". Most of the time it did, which I have shared and proved to certain people later on in my life by telling them what has been said, and then waiting for the proof to arrive in the not too distant future.

I have always picked up on people's true inner feelings, emotions and physical pain, just by standing near them and tuning into their Auric field. This is a magnetic

do the same if you are going to a place to which you have never been before, e.g. a meeting, an interview, etc. Try to visualize how many people are going to be there, what will be in the room in the way of fixtures or fittings, what colour the room is (floors, walls, furnishings, etc.) or try to tune into one particular person. Have a go at it, what have you got to lose? Practise makes perfect as they say!

4. There is one other method that I find useful for opening up your mind, and that is ESP (extra sensory perception). You can practise this by using cards. To start with use nine cards, any cards will do, whether playing cards, tarot cards, angel cards or even homemade ones with your own symbols drawn on them. Give them a shuffle without looking at them and place them face down. Have a piece of paper and a pen to hand. Now concentrate on each card and write down what you think it is. When you have written down all nine, turn the cards over and check how many you have got right. You can do this exercise as many times as you like. The more you practice, the more you will open your mind and the more you will get right. Go on you can do it! When you are getting most of, or all nine correct, move on to using twelve. You can also choose one of the twelve cards without looking at it, give it to a

it had something to do with the work that I would eventually undertake for spirit. (I will leave you to make your own mind up on that one). All I know is that once I started to open up and work for spirit, I never heard it again. So this goes to show, once the penny has dropped with us, spirit don't have to keep on repeatedly telling us. As I've grown spiritually, I have seen my life for what it is - a huge learning curve, and the quicker I learn my lessons the more work I seem to be doing for spirit, almost like passing exams.

The year of my twenty first birthday, my best Nan ever passed away, this dealt me a massive blow, as I hadn't seen her for a while before she died (for reasons far too complex to go into). I couldn't forgive myself for this for a long time, this made me enter into the same state of mind as when David had died, only it didn't last as long, probably because I knew for certain that there was a new life waiting for her, one without illness and pain, and one that would put her back with the people she had lost. From time to time I would feel my Nan's presence; often I would talk to her. I felt that, along with David, a little piece of my heart had gone with them, but that was ok, they more than deserved a piece of me, as I had been lucky to have them around me on earth for all the time that I had, and I knew that they would still come to visit me but in spirit form instead of in the physical. As I moved on in life I found myself working in jobs that I didn't really like, like most people I worked at whatever job I could get just to earn a wage at the end of the week.

I loved being with likeminded spiritual people, and I loved sitting in the energies of the spiritualist churches. The first medium I met that really impressed me with the way she worked, was a medium who when myself and my friend Carol went to see her at her house, she had connected mostly with my brother, and my Nan was in the background. David gave us no end of proof of his existence in the spirit realms. I re-call the expression on my friend Carol's face. At one point her eyes where bulging so much that she looked like a rabbit caught in the headlights of an oncoming vehicle. I thought it was great, apart from when she told me David said that he was a little lonely when he had first passed over, but now he had made friends and found people. As far as I'm concerned, and what I have been told and shown by my doorkeeper, family members and/or friends are waiting for those that are coming to the spirit world because they know before us when they are going to pass. This comment did hurt a little but I can only assume that David meant he missed his friends and family here on earth which made him feel lonely at first, but I thought as long as he's ok now, that's all that matters.

David had also come with some warnings for me which I knew in my heart were right before he gave them. There again was the confirmation from a medium's mouth, which I knew he had been telling me for a while. Being told

silently murmured "Hello", and 1 felt that they were pleased with the acknowledgement. I never felt as if I was being held back when climbing the stairs again after that.   Nick on the other hand was still experiencing this feeling, so I said to him "just say Hello, even if you just say it in your head, all they want is for you to acknowledge them". A few weeks passed and Nick hadn't said anymore about it, so I asked him if he was still getting that feeling, and he said "no", then he admitted to me that he had said "Hello" to the spirit as he was walking up the stairs one day, and guess what, that was the last time he had had that feeling too. At that time Nick worked night shifts some weeks, so at about midnight I would take Wesley out for a walk. Almost every time 1 walked back into our house, I could feel someone in there. I know that's a silly thing to say. What I actually mean, is that the energies were so strong at times in that house, that it felt like a living person was there. Bearing this in mind, a couple of times I went looking under the bed, in cupboards, behind doors, etc. with a heavy object in my hand just in case,. How silly did 1 feel! I bet the spirits in that house had a right laugh at me. Never mind 1 soon got used to them.

My brother used to come and visit but I only ever felt him in the kitchen. It was as if some of the former owners wanted the rest of the house to themselves. I was aware of an elderly lady called Eva, she was a real love, such a lovely

science. The doctors couldn't believe that he was still alive, as he had started to fade after about seven months. Eventually he asked them what was wrong, and of course the doctor had to tell him, that's when he really started to go downhill, we used to take it in turns to go and help him. One day Nick and I would go around, then the next day my Mum and Dad would go, this went on until in June 1992 when he died in hospital. But he had his last wish, which was that he would stay in his home until the very last minute, he was carried into hospital at around noon, and died just after ten on the same night.

At that time I was twelve weeks pregnant with our first son, Kial, (and yes I did know I was having a boy) and thinking to myself, that Grandad was just six months away from being a great Grandad. He was certainly already a very great Grandad in my eyes, if you know what I mean. He was a very strong, hard working, lovely Grandad, who was on occasions stubborn, so rumour has it, that's where my Mum and I got our stubborn streak from. I missed him just like I missed all the rest that had gone before him, but at least I knew he was with Nan, David and the rest of his family. At the age of eighty he had, had a very full life. He never sat around, until he had no choice, he was always helping others, and usually people older than himself; he was a man to be admired.

LIVING WITH NON-PAYING LODGERS

In December 1992 along came our first son Kial. All went fine; he was over 9lbs, healthy and loud. Then in 1994 I fell pregnant again with Callum. The pregnancy and his birth were to be a nightmare; as soon as he was born he had breathing problems. He went really pale and looked like his lips were turning blue. They rushed him off to special care, and there was nothing I could do. I felt completely helpless and beside myself with worry. For a few days we weren't sure whether he was going to make it, but he was a fighter. I too was very poorly after having Callum.

I remember one night when the doctors were trying to put another line in me, they couldn't find a vein as my body was starting to go into shock. Throughout the pregnancy I had suffered from kidney disease, asthma, and bowel disease causing a fair amount of blood loss and to top it all off they had used forceps in the c-section to get Callum out. This had caused my bowels to go on strike and my stomach started swelling. The pain was unbearable, I just didn't want this anymore, I told them all to leave me alone and they made it very clear to me that I would be very poorly indeed if they didn't get this line in. I still insisted they leave me be, I felt like a piece of meat but that's when I experienced my first healing miracle.

My body seemed to slow down completely; to the on-looking nurses I must have looked as if I had nodded off almost straight away. I remember my body feeling very

more proof of survival after this life, but he would not tell me about it at the time. As we closed for the night I took this thought with me and wondered what would happen. Well I didn't have to wait very long.

On the Sunday I trotted off to the local supermarket, whilst Nick stayed at home with the lads. When I returned home Nick was sat on the settee, with an amazed look on his face, he said "you'll never guess what just happened", and he proceeded to tell me that he had put a video on for Kial, and it was half way through, so he had stopped it, rewound it, and pressed play again on the remote control. So I'm stood there saying "yes, and", then he went on to tell me that it wouldn't play, so he turned over the remote to mess with the batteries (sometimes this made it work) when he discovered that there weren't any batteries in there (this often happened in our house with two small children about). "So tell me how the video player had stopped and rewound exactly when I had pressed those buttons?" he said. I just shrugged my shoulders and walked into the kitchen grinning to myself saying "thank you Michael for doing that".

It's not that Nick didn't believe in spirit, it's just that it didn't float his boat, and he really disliked the fraudulent mediums and the way they preyed upon peoples' misery, but by this happening to Nick, it kept him sweet, not that he minded me doing what I did, but he didn't at times see why I was so into it, (or it was so attached to me)!

searched it, he couldn't believe his eyes, I just smiled, and said in my head "cheers mate". Connor was cheeky like that. I could feel him laughing with us. Bless him, he had died a few years before in a tragic accident, but was still as large as life.

5

DOING MY BIT

When the children were very young I was involved in the running of a local spiritualist group. Once a month we would have an evening of clairvoyance, and after a few months we started workshops and events were held every two weeks.

I absolutely loved it, after each evening and event I would look forward to the next. I would open up the local village hall and set out the room ready for that evening's event. Sometimes I would chair the medium, this term means standing in front of the audience and introducing the medium, then when the medium has finished doing their address and demonstration thanking them for coming etc., giving the announcements for forthcoming events, closing the evening and directing the congregation to the tea and biscuits once the raffle had been drawn. I met some wonderful people doing this work. On one of the workshop nights we were running, the guest medium decided to base the workshop for that evening on finding out who our doorkeeper is. My colleague Ella and I, who ran the group, decided to sit in on this one. I had seen glimpses of my door

comfortable with and out through your mouth again for the count of two or four.

Feel your whole body begin to relax, relaxing more and more until you are completely at ease. Let your mind go with the music. You can imagine that you are sitting in a favourite place, upon a beach, in a field, besides a river, in a wood... anywhere in which you would feel comfortable and relaxed. Now let your mind drift wherever it wants to go and enjoy, but try and keep everyday thoughts out. Whenever your mind wanders back to everyday thoughts, concentrate on a still pond of water and go back to within that still space in the meditation. Enjoy the meditation wherever it takes you and whatever you see or feel. When you are ready to come back, do so slowly. Become aware of the chair upon which you are sitting, open your eyes and take a big stretch. If you do not feel completely grounded (light headed), having a cup of tea and eating a biccy can do the job, or you can stamp your feet up and down a few times.

As you start feeling more confident with your meditations, you can start linking with spirit if you feel ready. Always ask your doorkeeper for their guidance and protection just before starting your meditation. Say something like: "Door keeper (name) please look after me

things that had happened to me over the years were mostly normal (regarding spirit that is). I remember sitting in some of the workshops thinking "that's been happening to me since I was little". You see as I said before I wasn't guilty of ever picking up and reading a book on this subject throughout the years. All that I experienced and all that I was taught was through spirit. So as you can see, what's written in these pages is what has happened to me and my opinion. Take from it what you will and keep what feels right for you. As this is not an exact science, and we all can experience and believe things differently from the next person.

During this year I lost yet another person very close to me. Five days before my thirty fourth birthday, my dear friend Vivianne passed away during the early hours of the morning. We had been very close for some years and we both knew that we'd known each other in a previous life. We had made a pact with each other, that whoever died first had to come back as soon as possible after passing to visit the one that was still here. Viv always said "I know there's something after, but I'm just not completely sure what", so that's when we made the pact. On the morning of 12th July 1996, Nick had returned from a night shift (he'd taken another job as the building work had dried up for a while). I had made the comment to Nick that I knew Viv had gone during the early hours, as I was woken in early hours of the 12th with the most beautiful music filling the room, which for a moment I thought was coming from next door, but it wasn't.

I could see Viv in my mind's eye, sitting and smiling at me, and saying that she was ok now. She looked great, unlike a couple of days before when I had visited her in hospital. I was lucky enough in between Viv's relatives coming in and out of her room , to spend half an hour with her alone. She told me she was scared. I said "don't be scared, it will be alright". As I held onto her hand with both of mine, I asked spirit for as much help as they could give, and I gave as much healing as I could. I even visualized calming colours leaving my hands and flowing into Viv's hand, climbing her arm and finding its way into her heart to help calm her. She turned to me and said "Thank you". At around eight in the morning I received a phone call from a mutual friend of mine and Viv's. Julie asked if I was sitting as she had bad news. I said "I already know she's gone". Julie said "how do you know?" I said "I just know". I left my comment there, as anything to do with spirits, etc. unnerved Julie.

There are some people that you feel privileged to have known. Vivianne was one of them. She has visited me often over the years since she passed, and like my family that also visit I have always enjoyed her being there. She was a very special person then, and still is now.

the navel and it opens, from the front of your body running through to the back.

4*th*: ***Heart Chakra*** - its colour is emerald green, its element is air. It represents Unconditional love, compassion, healing and warmth. Its position is in the middle of the chest, and it opens, from front through to the back of your body.

5*th*: ***Throat Chakra*** - its colour is mid blue, its element is ether. It works with communication, expression, creativity and the ability to speak your truth. Its position is in the dip of the throat the area where the collar bones meet, and it opens, from the front through to the back of your body.

6*th*: ***Brow Charka*** - otherwise known as the 3rd Eye – its colour is violet, its element is light. It works with conscious perception, higher mind, intellect and intuition. Its position is in the middle of the forehead, and it opens, from the front of your head running through to the back.

7*th*: ***Crown Chakra*** - its colour is white or gold, its element is thought. It works with awareness of the eternal self, connection with higher energies and self realization. Its position is on the top of head, and opens upwards.

CHAKRA CLEANSING & BALANCING

First of all make sure that you are sitting in a warm and comfortable space, where you won't be disturbed for a while (phones off etc.). Put some relaxing music on if you want. When you are sitting comfortably, close your eyes and visualize roots growing out of the balls of your feet and into the earth or your feet sliding comfortably into mud to keep you anchored. Then take a couple of deep breaths slowly in through your nose and out through your mouth (the same as in the meditation).

Then starting at the base chakra and working your way up to the crown, visualize the colour of the chakra and the chakra opening to a medium width that feels right to you, rotating at a medium pace, clockwise, then pour pure white cleansing light into the chakra, swilling it around the chakra until you feel its cleansed. Then visualize pulling the white light back out again. As you pull the white light out imagine you are pulling all the negativity out with it, i.e. Visualize the base chakra as a red circle rotating at a medium pace in a clockwise direction and opening up as it rotates (the base and crown chakra's form a trumpet shape of light when open, the base pointing down the crown pointing upwards) until it reaches a size you are happy with maybe four or five inches then send a beam of white cleansing light up into the chakra, thinking I am sending this healing white light to cleanse my base chakra. Then pull it back out in a downward direction at the same time imagining that you are pulling all the negativity out with it. I usually do this three times on each chakra, then move onto the sacral chakra. Again visualize it as an orange circle rotating at a medium pace in a clockwise direction and opening up as it rotates until it reaches a size you are happy with maybe four or five inches (the sacral to the brow chakras run like a tube through the body from front to back, then open into a trumpet shape) then send a beam of white cleansing light through it from front to back. As you send it think I am sending this healing white light to cleanse my sacral chakra and as you pull it out the back imagine pulling all the negativity out with it. Repeat this with each chakra in turn. Always work from base chakra up to the crown chakra. When you have finished working on the crown chakra, bring yourself gently back to the here and now, make sure that you feel grounded. You can do this as much or as little as required.

You can do a lot of work with your Chakras and Auric field. Another exercise, that requires working with a willing friend or partner, is as follows:

get on, I wouldn't be without it. Also whenever you are working with spirit always ensure that you ask your doorkeeper for protection before starting any exercises.

You will get to know when to apply more, and if you decide to go into this kind of work, follow this path or are being taken along it, just like I have, you will find that protection is a must. A good tester on this subject if you doubt the efficiency of protection is try it for a week, morning and night, keep a written log of what differences it has made to your life, health, sleep etc. and then leave it off for a week, and compare them, see what you think.

As the first anniversary of starting up our spiritualist group came around, we had a wonderful first anniversary party and get together, we had a well reknowned local guest medium, who did us a fabulous demonstration of clairvoyance, followed by a buffet which we laid on, I re-call we had a great turnout for this event.

Unfortunately I was only to stay a few more months with this group after this time, due to further ill health from my ever deteriorating kidney and my family commitments, it became hard for me at this time to continue with the running of things, I was gutted, but I knew everything happened for a reason, so I waited to see what that reason would be. A good part of my life at that time was taken up with bringing our

6

SOME LOSSES ARE HARDER THAN OTHERS

As 1996 drew to close, I started to realize just how tired I had become, during the week with both of my boys being so young. I would go over to my Mum and Dad's a couple of times every week, they would keep the boys occupied whilst I made the most of a cup of tea and a rest. Then every Thursday Mum would come with me to Kidderminster to do the food shopping, it really helped having her with me, we had done this since Kial was born, it was our time together. Dad used to stop at home and get some paper work or DIY done.

Then one morning, at the beginning of December, when I was driving over to Mum and Dad's, the lads were making the usual amount of excited noise in the back of the car, as I had told them we were going to Nan and Grandad's. I had just reached about half way, and I was breaking to go round an island, when I experienced the vilest feeling go straight through my body. It entered my crown and dropped down to my feet, it was accompanied by the words "what if your Mum was to die?" My eyes instantly started to fill up. I said to myself "what on earth was that?" But I knew what 'that' was. It was the only warning I was to have of what was to follow less than two months later. For the rest of the journey, I just could not concentrate. I kept telling myself "don't be silly, it's just your mind playing tricks on you." I just didn't want to admit it to myself. As I arrived at my folks' house I must have looked in shock at what I had experienced, despite my best attempts to compose myself, Mum said "what's the matter with you?" "I'm just tired," I answered.

I kept looking at Mum and thinking, "no, nothing's going to happen, she's the best I've known her to be for years" (as she had really suffered with her health for a considerable amount of years). As much as I tried to file what had happened to the back of my mind, it just wouldn't stay there. Over the next few weeks we got ready for Christmas; Mum still had her health problems, but she seemed ok.

Christmas day was lovely. Mum and Dad came over for dinner, and then Kial's fourth birthday followed on the 28th. On the 29th Nick and I decided to have a party, our first one since the lads were born. I asked my folks if they would have the lads overnight, as young children and drink should not be put together as far as I'm concerned. Of course my Mum said yes to having the lads.

The next day I remember thinking to myself, "that was a great night". A brilliant get together with people we hadn't seen much of for ages (it had been a real laugh), and

"ring your Dad". Then just as I was considering doing just that, the phone rang and sure enough, it was Dad. He said, "the hospital has just phoned and said we had better go in, your Mum's taken a turn for the worse".

The time from leaving my house, collecting Dad and going over to Worcester Hospital seemed to take forever. When we finally arrived we were greeted by two doctors trying to explain to us that Mum had arrested just outside A & E in the ambulance. They explained that she had lost a lot of blood, and was currently in theatre. They wouldn't tell us any more than that though. Hours passed and Dad kept saying to me "she'll be ok, she's been through worse." Dad was just trying to make me feel better. I didn't have the heart to tell him what I had felt. I knew she had gone. I had felt her leave. I felt completely empty. As more time passed they finally wheeled Mum into intensive care. She was connected up to every tube and wire imaginable and she was also hooked up to a ventilator. I think Dad thought that she had made it this far, so she was going to pull through. I made sure Nick came and picked him up and took him home as he hadn't slept for days and he looked awful.

I sat by Mum's side holding her hand knowing she wasn't coming back. The nurses said "you should talk to her, just because they don't respond doesn't mean to say that they can't hear you." I thought to myself, "I know she can hear me, but not from inside that body." I think I sat there to give

but I lost some considerable time out of my life, which I have never gained back. There are parts of the kids lives following the death of my Mum that I have completely lost. In fact for a couple of years after I really don't know where I was at times. I just seemed to go through the motions, although I will say that I did feel Mum around, and even knowing what I know to be true, I still craved the physical connection. The most comfort I drew from this was that she had now been reunited with David. My Dad also felt this way. It was incredibly hard for him as they had never been apart since marrying. They had known each other since she was fourteen, engaged at seventeen, married at twenty two and she died at sixty three. I was just thankful after all the pain she had suffered in her life, that it was quick at the end.

So it just goes to show even if you know it's coming, some losses are harder to bear, why? I think it's mainly because even if we know they have gone to a better place, are happier and or pain free, with loved ones etc. Even if we are still able to feel the spirit of that person around us, communicating with us, we had such a love for them that we miss their physical presence, it is our loss of their physical company that we really miss.

7

GETTING DOWN TO SOME WORK

A year after my Mum died I started a cleaning and home help business up. I had a few people working for me, I loved the home help side, especially working with the elderly, most of them were a mine of information and life experiences, and I respected their decision to be so independent and stay in their own home.

I seemed to pretty much get on with earning a living and family life, but spirits were never far away. I would feel my elderly clients' deceased relatives around drawing close to my clients on a regular basis, especially just before they were about to pass over themselves, and a few did pass over in the time that I knew them.

Within this time I worked quietly with spirit, trying to put my relationship and understanding with them on a firmer footing. I would sit with likeminded people from time to time, and give people messages now and again, I would have medium friends over to my house to give people readings, just a bit of a get together I suppose, and at one point it became quite a regular thing. I thought at that point I

yourself comfortable by the side of your doorkeeper, speak to them with your thoughts and get to know them, stay there for as long as you like, when you are ready to leave, your animal will guide you back to the golden bridge, with every step you take over the bridge you can feel your body getting heavier, as you step off the bridge, you turn and wave to your animal, for they will be there waiting for you, not always the same one, but you will be greeted by an animal whenever you choose to go back. As you stroll up the narrow path and back through the gate into the field, you start to become more aware, now bring yourself back into the room, be aware of the chair you are sitting on, and take a big stretch. Make a mental note of how you thought it went, what you saw or felt and see how much progress you can make, remember, be patient, sometimes it can be a while before they will show themselves fully to you, they know when you are ready to move on, this doesn't mean to say that they are not working with and for you. When you come out of the meditation thank your door keeper for working with you and close down.

In March 2001 I finally had my kidney removed. Life had become a struggle at times before this, but I instantly felt better as soon as the operation had been performed. Then Dad was rushed into hospital three weeks later, and then

I think he was just a little frustrated being cooped up in hospital for five weeks. He just wanted out, and to get on with some sort of life. He'd said "they've sorted me out now, I just want to go home". That was the last conversation I was to have with Dad. At 6.10am the next morning, 30th July 2002, he collapsed and died of heart failure. Although I had expected it, it still came as a huge shock, especially when I received the news from the hospital over the phone. Unlike when Mum passed, I didn't feel Dad pass. I feel this was because I'd known for some considerable time (over 12 months) that Dad was going to pass away. Nick drove me to the hospital. Dad was in a room by himself. He looked just like he was sleeping. I went in and kissed him goodbye just as I had done with Mum.

I immediately started seeing to the funeral arrangements, which Nick found strange, but I'm best kept busy at certain times. Doris took it badly and I know she still misses him even now, she was an absolute star with my Dad, she was a good friend, and took a lot on herself when Dad was ill. I really don't know what I would have done without her. After Dad's funeral I can remember feeling like an orphan, very strange, but that's how I felt.

I may not have felt my Dad pass, but I will say he seems to be the first one through most times when I sit, and he draws very close to me at times. He had a very strong character when he was here, and nothing has changed now he's passed. I could imagine Dad as they open the doors, he would be saying "out the way please I need to speak to my little girl".

I re-call one afternoon I was visiting Dad in hospital, three weeks before he died, and just as I was leaving he gave me a peck on the side off my face and told me he loved me. You are probably thinking "yes, and...?", but the truth is, my Dad had never kissed me or told me that he loved me before that - ever. It's not that he didn't, it's just that we just weren't that sort of family. Funny as it may seem to some folk that was my biggest indication that there wasn't much time left, but Dad's actions that day made me feel very special. The months that followed Dad's passing felt pretty lonely. Somehow, I carried on being a housewife and mother, but inside I felt that another piece of my heart had gone with Dad. "Now," I said to myself , "pull yourself together, you've got Nick and the lads here, and over there Mum, Dad and David are all together in their family unit." But I missed them all (that's their physical presence I mean). I often feel their spirit presence, sometimes separately, sometimes together, but it isn't the same as going for a cup of tea at their house. I know one day though I will be joining them for that cup of tea, and it won't be here on earth, but until then there's work to be done, places to go and people to help.

Shortly after my Dad's funeral I saw a medium friend of mine, Nigel, who had given me a read a while before. He

8

PHASE TWO & THE ANIMALS

Towards the end of 2003, Nick's Dad was rushed into hospital as he had suffered more mini strokes, and he seemed to go off his legs completely. He also found it difficult to speak. He was placed in a hospital near to home (due to Nick's Mum's recent fall, she was unable to care for his Dad). So on Christmas Eve he was transferred to a nursing home with around the clock medical and nursing care. You could tell by his eyes that he didn't want to be there, but by this time he was unable to move or speak.

Two days after Nick's birthday on Sunday 7th March 2004 at 10pm, his Dad passed away. This hit the whole family hard and little did I know how much of an impact it would have on Nick for some considerable time to come. Nick's Dad was buried on Cheltenham Gold Cup Day (18th March). A number of his relatives had made the journey over from Ireland. He would have loved that as we had taken him to Gold Cup Day some years before. I could feel Nick's Dad around a little soon after he passed. I could even feel him around Nick when he was working on certain jobs, which was

When he sadly died at about eleven years old from cancer, it was like we had lost a member of our family (well we had really, hadn't we). A while after I bought another cat, when I got home we noticed he'd got extra toes on his front paws, so we called him Mittens. I seemed to sort of take to him and him to me, if you know what I mean. It was just like he had lived with me before, it really did feel like Wesley reincarnated. It wasn't only me that thought this, a good friend of mine, Maria, had never really taken to cats but she thought the world of Mittens and she thought he was Wesley too. When he was tiny he used to lie around the back of my neck even when I was walking around. He had perfect trust in me just like he'd known me before. He would follow me everywhere and come to bed with me, and still does. He seemed to be able to read my thoughts and mine his. I've proved this to myself time and time again.

PET'S PSYCHIC ABILITY EXERCISE

Try this little exercise, to see how much your pet picks up on your thoughts, you might be quite amazed at the results, if it's a cat you have and they follow you to bed like Mittens, when they jump up on the bed, try telling them where you want them to lie, e.g. Mittens sometimes tries to sleep too close to my head and purrs that loudly for ages that I can't get to sleep, so when he jumps up I tell him in my head (thought transferral) to go and lie down the bottom, it works most times unless he is being defiant, it works every time with Molly my other cat, she's extremely tuned in. See what response you get from your pets in different situations, I also find that when I meditate or self heal with Reiki that the cats in particular will lie very close to me, and seem to love the energies.

On Saturday 30th October 2004, I was sharing a coffee and a chat with Doris (my Dad's friend) when I saw in the local paper, a house for sale in our area, slightly larger than ours. It needed work doing but was brilliant for further extension as well. Our house had already been on the market for six months, we had been looking for some time as our two bed Victorian terrace had become too small. The following week we went to view it a couple of times and although our house wasn't sold we put in an offer and it was accepted. Within the same week we sold our house after so long on the market. Talk about how some things are meant to be.

As we set about the thankless task of packing and cleaning, the spirits in our house knew we were going, and I must say I felt watery eyed the day we left as they had been company to me at certain times when I really needed someone. One spirit in particular, called Eva, had been such a lovely energy. I had found out that she had lived there

sleep. With that I stood up and Nick said "where are you going?" with a worried look on his face. I said "I'm going to the toilet if that's ok". I know Nick well enough to understand if he thought the voices were that of a living person he would have been up there like a shot, but I could tell by his face he really couldn't understand what he had just heard, and had no intention of going to find out, so off I trotted upstairs.

As I entered the front bedroom, which I do believe was the last resident's resting place of a night, I found both kids sparked out, so I tucked them in, and off I went to the bathroom. When I returned to the living room, Nick said "well, are the kids ok?" "No" I said as I settled back down on the settee, "they are levitating around the room". Needless to say Nick didn't go upstairs for a couple of hours. The next morning I asked Nick exactly what he had heard and as he always does he said "nothing".

On another occasion I walked in the front bedroom to tuck the kids in and I heard someone groan and then moan. I got the impression that the man who lived here before felt pretty much like that towards the end of his life. I murmured "bless you", as I walked out of the bedroom, as I felt that all he wanted was to be acknowledged. I never heard him groan again.

I felt that he and his wife had been totally devoted to each other, and had been very happy together in their home. It must have been very lonely for him when his wife died, but

IT'S A KIND OF MAGIC

When it came to doing the clean up on the house after all the building work had been completed, Kirsten and her daughter came to help. As I knew that Kirsten picked up on energies, I asked her to see what she could feel, and "yes" just as I suspected she picked up on him. I will say at times I felt as if he was following us from room to room, bemused at the amount of work that had been done, and I knew that he had done very little on or in the house for some years before he died. I have often wondered whether the people that bought the house have felt his presence at all.

9

MY HEALING PATH

With my deteriorating health I started to look at alternative methods of healing, as I felt this would hopefully be of great benefit to me. A friend of mine had given me a business card for a lady in the Midlands, who was a Reiki Master. I did not know an awful lot about Reiki, but I had heard from a lot of people that it was amazing, and that it works on all levels of your body (the physical, mental/emotional and spiritual), so I thought I'd give it a go.

I booked an appointment with Lyn (the Reiki master whose card I had been given) in November 2005. Lyn was very friendly and made me feel instantly at ease. The healing session lasted for just over an hour but I was there for a couple of hours in total. When I climbed off the couch I felt the most relaxed I had done in years. Before I left we made another appointment for January 2006, and Lyn made the comment to me "go with the flow of things over the next couple of weeks". I didn't really know what she meant, only that maybe, like with a lot of holistic therapies, you can get a healing crisis shortly afterwards, but it only usually lasts a

this way of healing was pretty amazing, just to lie on my bed and feel the Reiki wash over and through me, just as if I was in Lyn's room.

Sensing Illness or Emotion in a Person's Aura

There is an interesting little exercise you can do at home with a willing partner, find yourselves a quiet space, play a little music for a few minutes to still the mind, don't forget to ask for protection of your doorkeeper, then one of you should be seated whilst the other slowly walks around the seated person, now the person walking around holds the flats of their palms about six to eight inches away from the seated person, take a mental note of what you feel, see etc; carry on with this for about ten minutes, and then change over, at the end of the session, sit down together and discuss what each of you have felt, seen, etc.

See if you picked up on how that person is feeling or where certain aches and pains, or problem areas are, I think you'll find this exercise fascinating, also when you go to visit a friend or relative, see how you feel when you stand close to them within their Auric field, see if you can detect any problem areas, even feelings of the emotional/mental kind.

- "Just for today I do not worry"
- "Honour thy teachers, parents and elders"
- "I will earn my living honestly"
- "Show gratitude to every living thing"

I think these are brilliant principles, and if we all tried to, at least some of the time, live our lives by these principles, we would help mankind and the planet we live on so much more than we do, and enhance our spiritual understanding.

In March 2006, I made the decision to close my business in order to follow my spiritual path full time. Working with spirit was the direction I had been dragged in for some years. The only person I couldn't give up looking after when I made this decision was a dear friend of mine called Joy. She was a relative of someone I knew, and although elderly, she was a mine of information and history, and she had somewhat become like family to me. Joy kept saying to me, "I would understand if you can't come anymore". It was there and then that I promised that I would carry on coming until she left her flat one way or the other. She used to say when people left there, it was either to be buried or go into a nursing home. She made a huge difference to my life, she seemed to understand me, and me her.

Joy was a very strong lady, and put up with a lot in the way of pain, but she never complained about it, she fully supported me in what I did, and she found it very interesting. Some days if I'd had reads to do the day before I saw her, the first thing Joy would say to me the next day was "how did it go yesterday?"

I would often feel the spirit of Joy's Dad in her flat, which she seemed to draw comfort from. So with Joy's support behind me, I set about concentrating a lot more on my spiritual path. My meditations seemed to grow stronger, my reads more accurate and my spiritual experiences more enhanced by the week. All through this year I carried on reading for people and spiritually healing, until one day a friend of mine asked for some healing. She was suffering with bad headaches and pressure in her head through stress, so I set about doing what I do. After about thirty minutes I finished, she looked at me and said "thank you so much, my headache feels much better, and I felt as if all this pressure was coming out through my ears". Now although I had done healing many times before, even on my children when they were very young, I had felt different after this healing session. I knew how to step into my protection and detach myself from the client and their emotions and or illness, but as the day drew on I started to feel more and more drained, until by the end of the night I really didn't feel well at all. In fact it took me several days to recover from that healing session.

energy stood in the corner of the room, this energy felt like it was of Egyptian origin and was very tall. I had learnt to accept energies being around me so all I thought was "ok, you can stand there if you want but I'm too tired to communicate, so if you want talk you'll have to come back some other time". With that I dropped into bed, and lay thinking this bed feels so good. Before long I must have dropped off to sleep, only to be woken by my whole body shaking, and then what felt like a huge electric current ran through it. I came to my senses very quickly. I recall saying out loud "what the bloody hell was that". From the foetal position I was lying in, I had turned onto my back and was just staring at the ceiling wondering in disbelief at what had just happened. Nothing during the experience had hurt me, it was just extreme, perhaps the most extreme physical experience I've ever had to date. Not being able to work out what had just happened or why, I soon dropped back off to sleep.

In the morning I awoke feeling refreshed and I pondered over what had happened to me the night before. I was very accepting of the bizarre, and I had learnt to go with the flow, but I just could not work this one out. So I picked up the phone and rang Lyn. I told her what I had experienced the night before and I waited for her response. All she said in return was, "you have opened more doors". Somehow this made perfect sense to me. From that day on it seemed that

more that spirit wanted me to do, so in February 2007 I decided to go for my Reiki Teacher's certificate. Now I knew that Lyn would not pass me until she knew I was ready. On the Teacher's certificate there's a lot more to take in and although the course was over two days like the others, Lyn made it clear to me not to assume I would pass within those two days. On the second day Lyn told me that she had been training another student for over a year before she was willing to put her name on a Teacher's certificate, so I didn't think for a second that I had passed within the two days. On the second day I was told that a woman who was doing her Master's certificate would be joining us, and that it was expected of me to give a Reiki meditation to her, like the one I had done on the first day, and that I would be called upon to explain certain things that fell within the Masters certificate (show teaching skills), within that day at a time chosen by Lyn. Then I had to go through the motions of how to carry out an attunement. Again Lyn had taught me this the day before, so as you can imagine that I'm walking around Lyn going through the procedure thinking to myself "I hope I'm doing this correctly, and how on earth does Lyn know what I am doing when she's sat there with her eyes shut?"

What came after all of this I really didn't expect, Lyn looked at me and said, "well done, you've passed". I jumped up and gave her a big kiss. At that very moment it was just as if someone had given me the world. I asked Lyn later how she had known that I was delivering the attunement correctly, her answer was "I could feel it". This comment I was beginning to understand having worked on other levels, but after learning the symbols that are placed into your Auric field when being attuned, you then can identify with the way the symbols are being placed in your aura, which ones they are and where, because you can feel the different energies of each symbol. I then asked Lyn why she didn't call upon me to explain anything to the lady who was doing her Master's certificate, she said "I didn't have to, as I was talking you joined in and I just let you take over and explain that point, and that was what I was looking for". Feeling over the moon, I went home with my Teacher's certificate in tow and a grin a mile wide.

was to place them in a sarcophagus, put the lid on, and they were expected to align their chakras and remove their spiritual body. Once the powers that be had evidence of this they would release them, and therefore they had passed the initiation test.

Lyn told me that I had been taken to this time to prove that I had passed the initiation test in this life, just as I had done in that life. I found all of this most fascinating and then I set about trying to find out exactly who I had been. To do this I went into this previous life a number of times either by Reiki regression, or sometimes spirit would just take me there in meditation. I eventually gathered enough information, including the letters of her name to research properly. I have enough knowledge about her now to understand more about certain feelings and experiences that I have had over the years.

In March 2007 we went to Luxor on a family holiday, but I knew it would be more than a holiday for me, as I stepped off the plane, I felt as if I'd come home. I know that sounds a bit of a weird remark to make, but I did. Ordinarily I don't care much for armed soldiers standing around, although it's supposed to be for our protection, they can be somewhat un-nerving, but I strolled through them as if they weren't there. As soon as we arrived at the hotel, I couldn't be bothered to unpack everything, I just had to go out and absorb the atmosphere. We were staying in a hotel on the

return flight I'm usually ready to go home, in this case that was far from what I was feeling. When we arrived home, I didn't feel tired from the travelling, in fact I was buzzing but laid back or to put it another way chilled out. Usually I run to the post open it all and start sorting out what needs to have my attention first. Not this time I picked up the post and filed it on the kitchen work top, and thought to myself "It will keep". This mood stayed with me for some time. To this day I still can't get over how my batteries felt so recharged, but in a much different way than I had ever experienced before. It was as if I had brought something back with me (which within the next few months it became clear to me that I had).

I seemed to gain a closer understanding as to what and who I had been exactly in that life in Luxor, and what my role had been. Bizarre as it may seem, is not unalike what I do now on the spiritual level. I do believe that she had a great insight some of which I've experienced and that she was a healer and held great respect and worked with higher energies. I know that in one regression I saw her holding a blue ball of energy in her hand, and that as she faded out of this life to pass to the other side, at the end of her physical life, it left her hand and floated upwards just as if it had been her spirit or the education and information that she had held so very close to herself for all of her life. That wasn't the last time that I would see that blue ball of energy.

WE'VE BEEN HERE BEFORE HAVEN'T WE?

On Sunday 6th May 2007, I had organised a coach trip to go to the Arthur Findlay Spiritualist College, where they have an open week once a year. There are various demonstrations throughout the day, mediums you can have a private read with, a healing room, stalls, gift shop, beautiful food and much, much more. It's a wonderful day out, and Kirsten and I have been going every year for a few years now. Only this year I took another 42 people with us. I re-call seeing a renowned medium, as soon as I sat with her she said that she saw me working up and down the country with my mediumship and also working abroad with it. She said, "I know what you're thinking, and it's the same as I thought many years ago... Why me? A little old housewife... the answer is why not you! If spirit want you to work in this way, you will". I must admit I did think "I cannot see that", even after all they had got me working doing one to one reads, healing, teaching, etc. I will also say those words have stuck in my head ever since, I suppose it's got to be someone. I just still couldn't see it being me, but this was one of the first warnings (for want of a better word) I'd had that I would be walking the platform in the future.

Following this trip to Stansted (which is what a lot of people call the Arthur Findlay Spiritualist College for short, as it is at Stansted) I decided to have another regression. This time I was taken back to 1872, where I had shared a previous life with Nick. I had been told this by a medium a few years

oranges, also with their segments. The tree we call our soul group, so you see when I passed to spirit side in 1957, I met up with my other relatives that have passed who belong to the same soul group (tree), and there I stayed in my little orange. I wasn't born again with the same spirit that had left that murdered lady's body in 1957. So if you have that feeling that you know that person from somewhere or you meet someone and get on really well with them from the off, or you meet someone and you are not so keen on them, because you seem to know something about them that you can't really put your finger on, don't rule out that you have walked this earth plane together before, and maybe more than once. Myself and Kirsten know that we have shared more than one life together, once as sisters, and once as mother and daughter (she was the mother). You can tell this, one because she is far more sensible than I'll ever be, two because she always tells me the truth, even if I don't want to hear it, and she would always try to guide me in the right direction, and because of these motherly qualities I do tend to take notice of what she says (well most of the time, see just like a daughter).

Over the years I have been reunited with many people I have known from previous lives, not always for the better. Sometimes I've been thrown back into their lives or them into mine for a reason, to learn a lesson or for karma to rebalance itself. I have found the whole subject of regression

HAVE YOU BEEN HERE BEFORE? EXERCISE

This is an exercise that all of us can do, you need to take time to recollect of how many times you have been to a place and have felt an affinity with it, or do the same with a person, take a few notes, and as life goes on see how much more you can add to your log, this takes time but you will amazed at some of the results and how all the pieces seem to start fitting together as time goes on.

As you progress with the depth of your meditation, try asking your door keeper for insights to previous lives and make a note of what you receive in meditation, keep a written log.

I believe there are also certain phobias, etc. that sometimes we carry forward from life to life, having a huge impact on us in this life. Most of the time these can be successfully removed using various methods such as Reiki or Hypnotherapy. This in turn enables us to move on and most of the time to fulfil our potential, whereas before we had been held back, maybe for years or even for all of our life.

We can also remove fears, suppressed emotions, sadness, etc., that have been a result of a trauma or a difficult period of time in our lives, whether it has been brought on by ourselves or others, whether this is from as far back as childhood or from later as an adult. I personally have experienced this as stated earlier in this book, I also know of many people that have experienced this themselves, some of which I have treated. There are no guarantees but there seems to be a high success rate. I find this work within Reiki is most rewarding, as I can see how Reiki has made such a difference to so many people's lives for the better.

In October 2007, I started treating a lady called Mary, who had had a phobia of cancer for what seemed like forever to her. It had started to really take over her life, she was all to consumed by her phobia, her waking hours were taken over most days with thoughts of the disease, not only could she not talk about or even mention the word at times, but she was starting to imagine all sorts of different cancers within her own body. At one time every pain or ache would worry her. She had tried other forms of healing including orthodox medicine, but nothing seemed to calm her worries, as soon as she started on the path of Reiki healing she instantly relaxed, even if it was only for the time she was on the couch, little by little over the next nine months she improved, sometimes falling back, when another little part of the phobia was taken away, but soon to recover the pace of moving forward. I knew with Mary that I was going to have move slowly and strongly if I were to make a long term difference.

I found that the phobia had been carried over from a previous life where she had suffered with the disease for

felt energy that dense before, and I haven't since. The most affected part of the house seemed to be at the rear of the property, both upstairs and down.

I decided to sit myself down in the lady's bedroom, where I was led to understand that the little boy had been seen a few times in the physical form. As I connected with this lovely lad called Sam, who was around ten years of age, he proceeded to tell me about his life, which wasn't all together brilliant. He was from the 1890's, and was a sort of runner for a low life scrooge type of business man (Arthur Daley character). His father had offered his son's services to this man, and he had to do pretty much as he was told. During the times when he wasn't being bullied, he was a happy child losing himself in his daydreams. To ease the pain of day to day life, including the pain of the back hander's that he got quite often for not doing things quickly enough. He told me that he had attached himself to this lady because he really liked her, she had gone past being scared after the first couple of sightings, as "he looked so sad, and inoffensive". The other reason for him for him being there so he told me, was because it was very close to where he had lost his life from one of those back hander's that knocked him of his feet and had resulted in him banging his head with fatal consequences.

I explained to him with the lady's permission that she didn't mind him coming occasionally to visit, but that it was

explained that he could see him wearing a blue jacket and a white shirt. Over the next few months every time she walked this route she could still feel this energy around this particular area, only it was getting stronger.

I was contacted by this lady shortly after, so I fixed a date with her to go over and see what I could do. As we were sitting in her kitchen enjoying a cuppa before our walk with her dog to the woods, and she was explaining to me that the energy only ever seemed to be in the same place, I had no knowledge of what her brother had picked up at this point or that they had both felt a hanging had taken place. With that I said to her, "I can see a man hanging from a Silver Birch, he is wearing a mid blue jacket, slacks and what looks like a white shirt, but as I look closer I can see a very thin lined check in the fabric". With that the lady's jaw hit the floor. She proceeded to tell me what she and her brother had felt and seen. I looked at her and said, "we best go and have a look then hadn't we?"

On went the wellies and off we went, with the dog in tow. As we approached the area, I had a strong feeling of not being able to breath, and then my head began to swirl. I decided to position myself up against a tree opposite the one he hung from. I could see an energy building up, I stood for a while with my eyes closed as I connected with the gentleman. When I opened my eyes I could see his energy standing in front of this huge Silver Birch tree opposite. I got the impression that he had hung from some considerable height. He proceeded to tell me that he had climbed so high up the tree, because if anyone did see him, he had to make sure that they could not get to him time to save his life. In other words, he meant to do it, he looked to be only in his late 20's, of slim build around 5'9" in height with mousey brown wavy hair. I had the feeling that the time he took his own life was around the 1950's, and he told me his name was Paul. He also told me that he had done it because there were parts of his life that he really couldn't cope with anymore, a big part of that was a lady he had had a relationship with, and that through some reason which wasn't disclosed it was not to be anymore.

I thanked him for coming forward to speak to me, and explained that it was his time to move on and to feel at peace now. There was no need for him to go on and keep torturing himself any longer. It was clear to me that he just wanted someone to know why he had taken his own life, with that I felt him fade gently. As we were making our way back, I said "I saw most of him, but not the colour of his eyes, because of having the image of him hanging". But just as I released those words out of my mouth, his face appeared in my head, with his eyes open, looking straight at me, "Oh", I said, in a shocked fashion, "they are hazel". Again I thanked him for his communication, and with that we made our way back.

EXTRA PROTECTION EXERCISE

If it's you that is starting to feel weird maybe a sick feeling, sensing something drawing close that you really don't like the feeling of, or being light headed, then putting your hand on your solar plexus and visualising a steel plate under your hand this will help. Also visualising yourself in a protective bubble or box with no entries or exits, and finally firmly asking the spirit to back off (when you do this you must really mean it, it's no good half heartedly asking the spirit to step away or the spirit may think you don't really want it to step away or back off). Sometimes you have to tell rather than ask, but I always do this with respect.

After a few moments, the feeling should ease off as the spirit steps out of your aura and your energies settle back down, you can do this as many times as you feel it is necessary, and as strongly as you feel it is necessary, I personally feel it is extremely important to apply protection before you arrive at any paranormal or such like events, I personally start applying my protection up to a couple of days before the event depending on what I feel I'm about to walk into, this can be either your own protection, asking your door keeper for protection or also asking the higher Angelic realms for protection, try one or

nanny/maid, and had she looked after a child there who had later died. It was her feelings for this child which were being revealed by using the lady who was over shadowed to show it. The rest of the night at Bordesley was very enlightening; all in all I had a fabulous time, thanks to the spirits of Bordesley Hall.

Moving on to Warwick Castle, I will say it has been to date the most exciting night for me that I have experienced on the paranormal front. This one took place on Friday 13th February 2009, once again it was another charity event with a world renowned medium. I find there's something quite magical about Warwick Castle, and at night it is just beautiful.

A couple of days before this event Kirsten had performed a regression on me through Reiki, which proved to be most fascinating. During one part of the regression I was on a white horse galloping across fields by Warwick Castle, so I had no doubt in my mind that one of my previous lives had been around the medieval times and somehow included some sort of link with the Castle. During another part of my regression I felt as if I was falling from a tower to the front of the Castle. The feeling was so strong it actually felt as if I was moving, and after the Reiki regression had finished Kirsten remarked that she had felt as if she was holding me down, well at least my spirit. This Reiki session was to unfold more than these lives, but more about that later.

I set about laying down my protection the day before the event and during a meditation I had. I was shown an Elizabethan man, who didn't look the sort of chap you would trust, he looked as if he was of some considerable wealth, but he happened to be stood in the dungeon. That's odd I thought at first but all was to be revealed. Then I saw all manner of different people, I was trying to make mental notes as they were shown to me. On the night we arrived at Warwick Castle I was excited. I always looked forward to visiting new places, and although I had been to the castle a few times before in the daytime, this was the first night time visit. During the course of that night we investigated the Watergate Tower (the Ghost Tower), and I discovered who the Elizabethan chap was. He was Sir Faulk Grenville, and he was stabbed to death by his servant come lover. The energies were flowing strongly in this tower, we didn't just have a dark shadow drift in, oh no it presented itself, or rather himself very close in front of us. Everyone in our group felt a lot of paranormal activity within the walls of the bottom of this tower.

Other brilliant places with lots of energies we found that night were the nursery within the main Castle, the corridor outside the nursery, the waiting room/corridor downstairs. We all picked up on an awful lot, including a

12

HELPING OTHERS ON THEIR SPIRITUAL PATH

I have always tried to help others on their spiritual path for as long as can remember, through the passing on what I had learnt though the years, whether that had been in workshops, circles or my own experiences.

This side of spirit work interested me and apart from helping Jane and others in the past with workshops and circles. I decided to hold some by myself, so I set up a series of workshops and circles, I had been teaching private lessons before this, which I will still do when required, but I felt that the workshops were the way I had to go.

So with spirits guidance I held my first workshops and circles. They turned out to be a real winner, good fun whilst at the same time learning. I have met some wonderful people through this work, and the more they developed spiritually the more it drove me forward to do more and the more I liked it, it seemed to give me a real sense of achievement when it all came together.

To open someone up and help them achieve their potential is a brilliant feeling. The workshops I do include

bed when I felt a presence in the room. As I turned over to face the door, I heard Tony's voice saying "don't be frightened , its only me, I've just come to see you, and tell you again that everything will be ok, and I'm fine, can I go and look in on the kids?" I answered "thanks for that, I'm glad you are ok, of course you can go and look in on the kids, and Nick's down stairs watching TV." With that the deep brown mist that had stood in front of the bedroom door drifted out onto the landing, bless him Tony had made that effort just to tell me that all would be ok , and it was, and to say he was ok, which I knew he would be. He was always interested in what I did, and I knew he would love the spirit world when it became his time, and that he would accept very quickly his passing and where he was.

Tony seems to come in an awful lot during times of teaching. He consumed a lot of fags in his life, and I can feel him watching what I'm teaching at times, and then I smell the smoke. It's good for the students too, as they often smell his smoke, and I just say "that will be Uncle Tony".

A lot of the time when I'm running a circle, I can often get the information on what spirit want the content to be within the circle that evening the very second I walk into the room to start the circle and not until then. This is how much trust you have to have in spirit. At first I used to feel very uneasy because of this, then as time went on I realised that they were teaching me a valuable lesson too, by making me trust them. Which is just the same as anyone else should do, trust in what you get and know that when they are asked spirit will deliver.

I found the more I pursued the teaching side of this work the more people were sent to me. But teaching in this way is not the only way of helping people on their own spiritual path. In June 2008, my good friend Joy passed after a short stay in hospital. For the few weeks she was in there I tried to visit her most days, and sat with her. Although she was unable for most of the time there to speak, she would communicate when she could by moving her fingers when I held her hand and spoke to her. As I sat sometimes for a couple of hours at a time, I would give her healing to ease her journey as I knew there was to be no recovery from her illness in this life for her.

As I sat with Joy, I could feel her family waiting for her. Her Dad had often been felt by me in her home, but now I could feel other members of her family around her waiting for her to come home. Some time before when Joy had talked about this subject, I said to her, "if you go before me then show me a sign, and if I go before you I'll give you a sign when I get to the other side." Joy said, "well I'm more likely to go before you, aren't I?" "You don't know, do you?" I said, as we both laughed, but Joy was to do exactly that.

On the day that she passed, Nick and I were in the living room when we both heard what sounded like a mini

teachers themselves. I had felt this for some time, and had started to put it into action, knowing full well who had to be the first (poor Jeanette). But the lovely thing is when we get our confirmation, you see I don't challenge what spirit give me, I just accept, but every so often I ask for a sign from them that I'm going in the right direction and doing what they have guided me towards, and on this occasion they had confirmed this by using a medium friend of mine.

Jane and I were sat in one of her workshops recently, all the students were giving each other reads with different sorts of cards, so we thought we would give each other a short read whilst they were busy and didn't seem to need our help. When placing the cards out, Jane said "I know your teaching is important to you, but they are telling me that you are going to teach the teachers, if you know what I mean". I smiled and said "yes, I know what you mean; I have one person already that they have told me I must teach to teach". So you see although I knew, it was lovely to have that confirmation.

I do find that I seem to be teaching in other areas of my life, spirit from time seem to throw me towards people that are very inquisitive towards what I do, whatever age they may be and from whatever walks of life they come from. I find people constantly asking me about all aspects of what I'm involved in, and spirit put me in the right place at the right time. So in a way this is spirits way of putting me where

13

MY ANGELIC FRIENDS

For as long as I can remember I can re-call another energy at my side, an energy not at all like spirit energy. This energy felt completely different, for a start with spirit I could usually see the person at least in my minds eye if not their energy in front of me, usually it felt cool (temperature) to me and sometimes their feelings became my feelings, but with this energy it was so very different.

I felt no earthly body had ever been attached to them, although I saw their energy in my physical eye of sorts. I never had an image in my mind's eye, I would, to start off with see a heat like energy rising with outstandingly bright flickers of white light, not like the flickers of light I had when spirit were around, the more I saw and felt the more they drew me, and I just had to find out more about this unusual energy which kept surrounding me.

Many years before when I was much younger these energies would make me a little nervous, as I thought they were no more than spirit, but when I tried I could never pick up who they were or what they wanted, so I spent a long,

long time just feeling that some weird spirit energy was following me around. As I didn't believe in Angels of any description then, I just thought they were either wishful thinking for people when times got hard, or belonged to people with very bizarre imaginations. How wrong can you be! I finally got to a point where I was feeling this energy so much and so strongly around me a lot of the time that I started asking more and more questions, "who or what are you? What do you want? Why do you keep hanging around me? Why won't you tell me who you are? I really need to know now, please reveal yourself, if you want to work with me now would be a good time to let me in on what you want". I asked loads of questions for a while until suddenly I started to get clear answers in the way of everywhere I went angels of one description or another were thrown in front of me, in shops, friends houses, hanging in car windows, on cards, on TV, radio, in conversation. I know what you're thinking, that it was just coincidence. Well there's no such thing as coincidences and until the penny dropped with me, which actually wasn't that long, I was flooded with Angelic everything.

As soon as I accepted the signs given to me, the signs became less. The best sign of all and the most fascinating was the perfect fluffy white feathers wherever I went they would be there. I would gaze out the window as I washed up, and yes there was another feather floating down gently in front of

the beginning of 2008, minding my own business watching TV. I started to hear "we need to talk to you" over and over again. As I was watching the end of my programme I chose to ignore it for a while, but the voice kept coming. So I said in my head "in a minute". It backed off until the end of the programme. After which I said to Nick "what's on now", and he turned it over to some boring spy documentary. At the same time the voice came back "we need to talk to you". I thought, "I give up", and said in my head "I'm coming", with that I proceeded to make my way to bed. Once tucked up, I decided to put a little music on. As I felt the Angelic presence draw even closer I closed my eyes. It was not needed for me to chill and open up and connect with them, they were already there waiting for me. As I lay there it wasn't long before I felt myself being lifted out of my body and taken to a place of unconditional love. That is the only way I can describe it. I knew the purpose of their visit that night was to take me to have a peek into where you go when your spirit leaves your physical body in death.

I could feel them taking me and walking by my side and behind me but I did not lay my eyes on them at all. It was a bluebell woods they had taken me to, and as I was strolling through these woods with them by my side I could see the colours were clearer, vivid, bright. I had never experienced these colours on earth before, it was like it was pure, and earth is so dense now I suspect the colours would

had just happened. I glanced at my watch, I had been in that wonderful place for not much less than an hour, and already I wanted to go back for another hour. As I lay there contented with my experience it had become increasingly clear why they had taken me there and why it was so important. They needed me and wanted me to understand what was there for us beings after the physical body had gone. Now I fully understood why they called it home.

As I carried on my work I understood when auntie Mary or Uncle Fred came through and said that they were happy where they were and were surrounded by the people that they had loved on the earth, and that we as physical beings should not worry about them because they were at peace. I do believe whole heartedly after my experience that this is exactly true. I feel they have more concerns for us, and try to help and guide us as much as they can.

The wonderful experience that I was fortunate enough to encounter that evening, I feel I will cherish until I leave this body to join the spirit dimension back home. I feel very privileged to have been taken by my wonderful Angelic friends for a preview, albeit momentarily. As my connection has continued and my relationship has grown with my Archangels , the energy I feel from them has grown in intensity too.

Recently I underwent a minor operation in hospital. For some strange reason the general anaesthetic knocked me for six this time. I have always been fairly ok afterwards, but this time I felt completely wiped out. The day after I came home I decided to have a meditation in my room, as I sat and chilled I could feel their Angelic presence draw closer. One presence in particular was much stronger than the others. I felt my crown chakra extend beyond belief, my physical heart started to bang as my heart chakra opened fully and an overwhelming heat surrounded me and seemed to enter my crown. As I opened my eyes fully I was met by a huge whirlwind of clear and electric purple energy rapidly approaching me. It was a powerful yet nurturing energy. Then I heard the words "you need to go and lie down, you need to rest", and with that I thought I'd better do as I was told. So I closed and thanked my doorkeeper and Angels for sitting with me and off I went. As soon as I climbed into bed, I must have instantly dropped off to sleep as I can't remember much after my head hit the pillow. About an hour or two later I was awoken by some of our friends who had popped round to see how I was. I sat up in bed feeling quite refreshed, which was unusual for me as I can never sleep in the day unless I'm extremely ill, and if I do, I never wake feeling refreshed, I usually feel worse, but on this occasion I felt as if my Angelic friends had been healing me whilst I was snoozing, and I felt quite well considering.

I retraced my thoughts to the one most powerful energy in my room earlier that day, I knew that it was the

But there goes another difference of opinion - some feel that angels can take on a physical form when needed (and even if they can or do it doesn't mean they have walked the earth as humans before). What's your opinion?

Do always learn to keep an open mind as none of this is an exact science. I have gained my thoughts and opinions over my lifetime so far and have searched for the answers, some of which I have been given, some of which I have found, and a lot of which I am still looking for. I have kept asking until certain things have made sense to me. I haven't taken anything for granted and I have learnt to listen to my own heart and mind on these matters. The best proof you can gain is not what you read or what other people tell you, but what feels right to you. If you always work from the heart and with love you may be surprised at what comes back to you. I will personally look forward to many more Angelic encounters in the future, and here's to knowing that our relationship will go from strength to strength on every level.

use them just like the cleansing and balancing exercises earlier. With the Chakra set everything is amplified. I have had some amazing experiences with my Chakra set. I feel the type of stones you choose is up to you, as long as they coincide with the colours of the chakras. Some people choose to research the individual qualities of each crystal they choose for their set but ultimately it is down to personal choice. My choice of crystals for the chakra set are:

- Base – Red Jasper
- Sacral – Carnelian
- Solar plexus – Citrine
- Heart – Green Aventurine
- Heart (left) – Rose Quartz
- Throat – Lapis Lazuli
- Brow/Third Eye – Amethyst
- Crown – Clear Quartz

As quoted earlier the Chakras run in a straight line, but as you can see above I've added an extra one (Rose Quartz), which I place over the physical heart. This was introduced to me by a friend, and works perfectly for me as I feel Rose Quartz is very much the heart stone. Some of the qualities of the crystals I have chosen are:

◎ **Red Jasper** - This stone grounds energy, it also stimulates the base chakra, it help to clean and stabilize the aura, this is a stone of health and is both strengthening and detoxifying.

◎ **Carnelian** - Can also be grounding but of high energy, excellent for restoring vitality and motivation, it has the ability to cleanse other stones (so a good one to keep in your chakra pack), it can help you to accept life and remove the fear of death, overcomes negative conditioning and encourages steadfastness.

◎ **Citrine** - Again Citrine is another stone that never needs cleansing, it is a powerful cleanser and charger, and a very beneficial stone, it is an aura protector, it has the ability to cleanse the chakra's especially the solar plexus, it can help to activate the crown and open the intuition.

◎ **Green Aventurine** - This crystal can defuse negative situations and turns them around, it promotes compassion and empathy and encourages perseverance.

◎ **Aventurine** - Stabilizes one's mind, stimulates perception, and enhances creativity. It is a comforter and a heart healer and a general harmonizer, protecting

If you would like to start by just cleansing the chakras, find a comfortable place to lie down (e.g. your bed), soft music helps, turn telephones off, choose a time and place where you will not be disturbed. I find a flattish pillow for my head works better than being propped up. Now lie flat on your back, with your legs together and place your first crystal in the 'V' of your groin. This is your base chakra and the colour is red. The next is the sacral chakra and the colour is orange. Place this crystal on your tummy in between the pubic bone and the navel. Then comes the solar plexus - the colour is yellow and the position is approximately two inches above the navel. Next is the heart chakra and the colour is green. The position is the centre of the chest. Moving on to the throat, the colour is blue and the position is in the dip of the neck where the collar bones meet. On to the brow/third eye chakra - the colour is amethyst/violet. The position is just above the eyebrow line in the centre of the forehead. And finally the crown - the colour is clear Quartz to me, and the position is on the top of the head in the centre. Your optional extra crystal is Rose Quartz and the position is on your left side of your chest. Some people prefer indigo for the brow and amethyst/violet or gold for the crown, whatever your preference on these two chakras, the bottom five have

exercise I have personally felt really quite well and centred. You can do this exercise as little or as often as required, as I think there's everything to gain and nothing to lose.

Another great way of working with certain crystals I find is within meditation. If you have progressed well with your meditations and feel ready to try something a little different, try sitting with an amethyst in your hand or hands. Some people say you should always hold crystals when working with them in your left hand, because it is closest to the heart, others say that you should hold them in your dominant hand, which could be your right hand. I say do what feels right for you, after all you are the one working with the stone. Amethyst has a high spiritual vibration and so can guard against psychic attack turning the negative energy into love and it enhances higher states of consciousness and meditation. It may also enhance spiritual awareness. These are just some of the attributes of Amethyst as well as the ones stated earlier, so as you can see it's a good one to start with.

Another way in which you can work with crystals is as follows:

CRYSTAL MEDITATION

Go through the same procedure as any other meditation; the only difference is that you are holding onto a crystal of your choice in this case Amethyst. Some people find this sort of meditation very strong where as others not so different to a normal meditation, as you glide through your meditation try to keep a mental note to how you feel...

Are your feelings any stronger? Are the colours you see any clearer, or are there more? Do you feel your Chakra's opening any wider? Do you feel that your Clairvoyance, Clairsentience or Clairaudience has become any clearer?

Always remember your grounding after, as stated earlier this sort of meditation can be a little or a lot stronger than a normal one. It's a good idea to keep your note book by the side of you and jot down straight away what you have experienced, then if you find yourself drawn to this sort of working, why not try Rose Quartz, I think this is a truly beautiful stone to meditate with, as stated earlier it is the heart stone and one of unconditional love.

I always found over the years that I would be attracted to certain pieces of crystal jewellery on certain days e.g. I found I would be drawn to put on Moonstone or Amber when I needed a womanly stone. If I was doing reads, I would put on

raved on about a crystal, when I've held it, I've felt nothing or next to nothing or on a couple of occasions I've not liked the stone at all. People say that you are attracted to what you need or what suits you at the time. I do think there's something in that saying. I have worked with other powerful crystals such as Tektite and Prophecy Stone. The Tektite was very enlightening and seemed to enhance communication with the higher realms. But the one to date that really did it for me was my Prophecy Stone. Again I'd heard a few things about these stones and was very drawn to them, so off I went to ask Dave and Maureen to source me one as I knew I could trust them to get me the real thing (as some people had been selling cheaper inferior stones and passing them off as Prophecy Stones). Maureen said to me that she had already got one somewhere - it was just a matter of finding it. Sure enough a few weeks later it appeared. I happened to be in the shop at that time giving a read to a lady. When I had finished Maureen showed me the stone and said "why don't you go in the back and sit with it for while before you buy it?" (as these stones can be fairly expensive). I looked at my watch and thought "why not, I haven't got to rush off any where", so off I went and sat in the back room. From the time Maureen had placed the stone into my hand I had felt excited about this one. As I closed my eyes and stilled my mind, I was thrown into what seemed like a future civilization. I know what you are thinking but that is what it looked like and the associated

this was the last class, I thought it would be nice to give the students a little something to take home and work with. So I purchased from my usual supplier a number of Amethyst polished tumble stones. When I got home from the shop I cleansed and charged each and every one of them using the Reiki symbol Choku Rei. As I handed them out around the circle there were a few raised eyebrows. I told them to hold the stone in whatever hand felt right to them. I also explained briefly some of Amethyst's attributes and why I had chosen this stone for them. The music went on and Jane talked them into a soothing meditation, guiding them into beautiful woods and letting them sit and drift as they hopefully opened to spirit and collected information from them for someone in the circle. With Amethyst in tow I knew it would enhance what most people picked up. Although I did note that some people felt no point to holding a stone. As Jane guided them back from their meditation with spirit and back to the here and now, there were surprised looks on a few faces. Most had had a wonderful and powerful time, and all but one person in the group felt that tiny Amethyst stone pulsating in their hand. Just like it had a little heart beat all of its own, they were amazed.

CARING FOR YOUR CRYSTALS

After the class I explained how to maintain the power of their stone, as all crystals absorb negativity. There are some that are self cleansing and self energising, however for the ones that need cleansing and charging there are different ways that this can be done. One of the most popular ways is to hold the stone under cold running water point down (if it has one) and say three times "may the negativity flow from you". Then turn it point up under the running water and say "may you be filled full of love, light and healing energy". Say both of these three times. My Reiki teacher introduced me to this method and really I think all crystals should be cleansed every time they have been used. Or if they haven't been used for a while, I will often just charge them up again before use. Not that they should need it after being cleansed and charged after use, but I've got into a habit of doing so, and I think this habit doesn't hurt.

Another popular way of cleansing/charging is to sit your crystal on a window ledge when the moon is out, as the moon will cleanse and re-charge your crystal brilliantly. I would personally just leave them there when the moon is out. Some people believe that the sun charges and the moon cleanses. I'll leave that one to you to make your own mind up. What I will say is please don't leave crystals in strong sunlight. One because you may just set your house on fire (this has already happened to a few people, as we all know clear crystals e.g. crystal balls etc., act as a magnifier), so don't risk it. Also you will find that the sun will fade some of the beautiful colours in your crystal. I purchased a wonderful

15

WHERE THERE'S A WILL THERE'S A WAY

As time has gone on I've loved every minute of working with spirit, but in 2008 they started to drag me in a different direction. They decided that they wanted me to 'walk the talk' and write this book. Indeed, I was told some five years ago by a well renowned medium that I would write a book. My first thought, as soon as I could stop laughing long enough, was "never, I have trouble stringing a legible sentence together sometimes, let alone write a book!" However, I kept thinking about this remark over the next few days, until I completely dismissed it. The only reason why I had given time to this thought in particular in the first place, was because of the person who had told me. I knew how accurate she was when she linked with spirit, "Oh well", I thought, "if it happens, it happens but somehow I don't think so as I wouldn't even know where to start". Little did I know spirit would be guiding me in my writing too. Again, about 18 months ago another renowned medium told me exactly the same thing, and again I thought "we'll see".

earlier, you'll find most times you will have what you are looking for within no time, that's unless you already know the answer deep down. Now this part sounds crazy, but I know there will be another book to follow this one at some stage. What it will contain I couldn't tell you as I don't know myself yet, but yes you've guessed it, spirit told me, so again I guess spirit will dictate the writing of most of it, just like with this one. What I do know and most certainly hope for is that it is going to help people advance on their spiritual path, just like I hope this book has assisted those who have taken time to read and participate in the exercises within its pages, and not to feel alone when they experience spiritual presence, however strange, weird and wonderful it may appear. As you can see I've had many strange, weird and wonderful spiritual experiences myself, a few of which have been stated, and may I continue to do so until I eventually go back home to them.

Now I do know that spirit have been preparing me for something more in the public eye for some time. So I know that helping Jane with her classes for some years and getting to feel comfortable in front of a number of people was no coincidence as was being thrown into doing a Mind, Body and Spirit fair. Being asked by so many people at one time to run my own spiritual development workshops I didn't feel like I could say no, giving talks in front of a number of people on psychic awareness, leading charity events, running circles, attuning people to Reiki, etc. All these things were no coincidence. In fact they have kept throwing me out of my comfort zone of one to one reads. Even going back to chairing the mediums and helping in the running of the local spiritual group all those years ago, I remember thinking then, it must be nerve racking for some of these mediums standing in front of all of those people. Well that was until one of those mediums said to me, "I'd rather stand here and work than do what you do, introducing me and giving notices, etc." This comment I didn't understand for some years. Then I started occasionally reading in front of more than one person at a time by request. Still I was in my comfort zone albeit stretched a little again. Then I was receiving a number of calls for me to do clairvoyance demonstrations. One call was from a spiritualist church not many miles away, so I agreed to be booked in. I had been asked by a more local church a couple of times in past years but for whatever reason I had declined. I suppose if you are asked for long enough you will eventually say "yes", as the asking doesn't seem to go away (where there's a will there's a way, spirit's will, spirit's way). I had also been asked to demonstrate at pubs and stand in for a well known medium who was ill at the time, all of which I declined. So you can see what was happening here - I was sent offers over and over again until I eventually said "yes". I know I would have started doing demonstrations years ago, if I had just said "yes" then, but spirit wasn't going to give up on me.

second before I stood. Once in front of the audience, spirit was by my side, the very ones that were in my room with me earlier. I only gave two messages that evening but I remember them being quite detailed and well received. As I sat back down, I completely deflated. At the end of the service we exchanged a few polite words with people and I turned to Jeanette and said "can we go now? I don't feel well". With that we left, I didn't even have a mince pie, one of my favourites. I remember that even climbing into Jeanette's car to go home felt like real hard work. As we made our way back to my place, we discussed how the evening had gone. I must say Jeanette lifted my spirits when she told me how well the messages had gone down from sitting in the audience herself. This made me feel happy about the way spirit was pushing me towards the platform, and I thought at least platform work re-unites more people with their loved ones at one time in one place, albeit momentarily. As soon as I arrived home I went to bed with more paracetamol and a bottle of water, but contented. You see where there's a will there's a way (spirit's will, spirit's way). If Nick had been in a better mood I wouldn't have gone, instead I would have curled up on the settee with blanket, tablets and water. Although I knew it had to be done, feeling so awful it was touch and go. As Nick came home in such a foul mood, he must have activated my adrenalin enough to go. However you feel sometimes, when someone's irritated you enough,

to any event. All I had in my head for a while was "when we need to be there, we'll be there". As I walked into the church there was still nothing. My friend Jane was also doing this evening with me and I stood in the back room with her and said "I've got nothing". "Don't worry", she said and just as Jeanette had stated on the way there, "they'll be there for you even if it's at the last minute, spirit will not let you down". And come to think of it, why would they if they want me to do this work? With that I walked out to face my audience. Still nothing there. Jane took the opening prayer and address, and then it was my turn to stand and deliver what I had. Talk about last minute, the very second I stood was the very second that spirit started. From nothing to everything in a second. Other mediums may be used to working this way but I never had. I'd always had spirit with me before arriving at an event.

Saying that, I hadn't at this point done a lot of platform work, and with my one to one reads, sometimes I had very little - if nothing at all before the client arrived. But once sat in the client's company before the read began, spirit would come through. And then on the other hand, sometimes I'd had some that were just waiting for their loved ones to come and see me for a read. These spirits sometimes had been with me for a few days before. I suppose being in front of an audience and still not receiving anything until I stood up there felt weird and a little scary if I'm to be honest, but just another lesson as far as spirit was concerned, and it was one of complete trust in spirit, and that night showed me that I could. I also learnt, as I've been nudged along the platform path, that some of the time they will be there when needed and not before. In the last year or so I have noticed a vast change in the way spirit and the Angelic realms work with me, and this is one of them.

As this year moves on I kind of know what they have planned for me, but that's another book. I have however learnt to go with the flow more and see where it takes me, accepting more invitations for platform work, as I know deep down that will be a part of my future work. I suppose part of my hold up has been that certain areas of my work have had to decrease and I have felt guilty for that, but as often you find out, and the hard way, you can't do it all at the same time as there aren't enough hours in the day.

I hope you find your spiritual path like I have found mine. If you have, nice one, and if you haven't yet, carry on searching as the fulfilment is worth the wait and the journey is one of excitement, and I hope you feel you can help others onto theirs, just as I hope I have. So until spirit and I move forward onto another book; ask the questions, wait for the answers, meditate, practise the exercises, listen to your higher consciousness, trust and accept what is being given, for that is how you will move on. You have got nothing to lose and everything to gain!

Today, she is a wonderful and very evidential medium, a Reiki Master/Teacher & Crystal Therapist. Janet runs her own workshops & development circles which are packed full of information and practical exercises, as well as giving Clairvoyance Demonstrations, private reads and much more.

To discover more about Janet and her inspirational work please visit:

www.janetocarroll.com

Lightning Source UK Ltd.
Milton Keynes UK
UKHW02f2031081117
312397UK00017B/1268/P